RICHARD ORR'S
NATURE
CROSS-SECTIONS

ILLUSTRATED BY
RICHARD ORR

WRITTEN BY
MOIRA BUTTERFIELD

DORLING KINDERSLEY
LONDON • NEW YORK • STUTTGART

A DORLING KINDERSLEY BOOK

Art Editor Dorian Spencer Davies
Designers Sharon Grant, Sara Hill
Senior Art Editor C. David Gillingwater
Project Editor Constance Novis
Senior Editor John C. Miles
U.S. Editor Camela Decaire
Production Louise Barratt
Consultant Simon Tonge

First American edition, 1995
2 4 6 8 10 9 7 5 3 1
Published in the United States
by Dorling Kindersley Publishing, Inc.,
95 Madison Avenue, New York, New York 10016

Library of Congress Cataloging–in–Publication Data
Orr, Richard.
Nature cross-sections / Richard Orr, illustrator;
Moira Butterfield, author. – – 1st American ed.
p. cm.
ISBN 0-7894-0147-9
1. Habitat (Ecology) – – Juvenile literature.
[1. Habitat (Ecology) 2. Ecology.]
I. Butterfield, Moira, 1961-. II. Title.
QH541.14.O77 1995
574.5 – – dc20   94 – 44798
                                   CIP
                                   AC

Reproduced in Italy by G.R.B. Graphica, Verona
Printed in Italy by L.E.G.O.

CONTENTS

BEAVER LODGE
4

TERMITE CITY
6

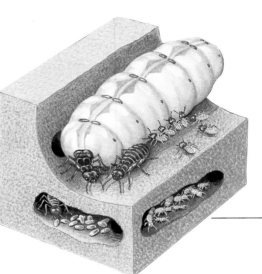

TROPICAL RIVERBANK
8

RAIN FOREST 10

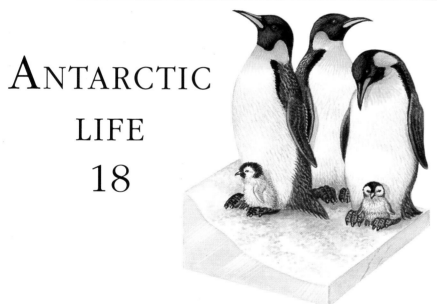

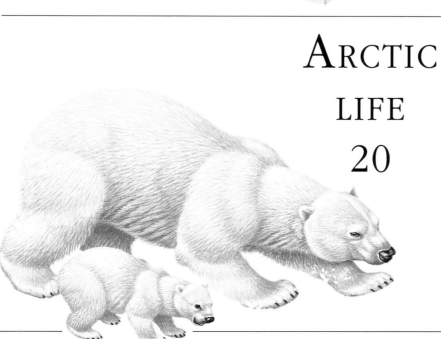
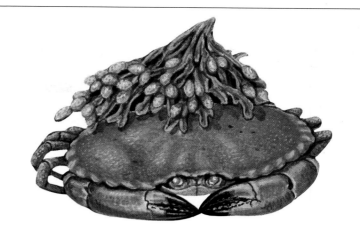

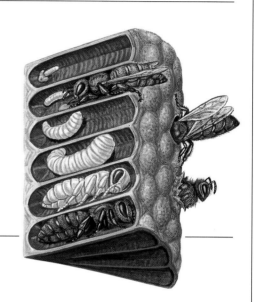

BEAVER LODGE

BEAVERS ARE AMONG THE MOST SKILLFUL BUILDERS in the animal world. These busy engineers are famous for constructing dams across rivers and streams. A dam holds the water back so that it spreads out into a deep pool. Here the beavers build their homes, called lodges. Inside, they are safe from enemies because all the lodge entrances are underwater – and even though it is built with branches and mud, the roof of a lodge is so strong that even a fierce, heavy grizzly bear would find it hard to break in. Beavers could once be found in wooded areas nearly all over the northern world. Now they are most common in Canada and the US.

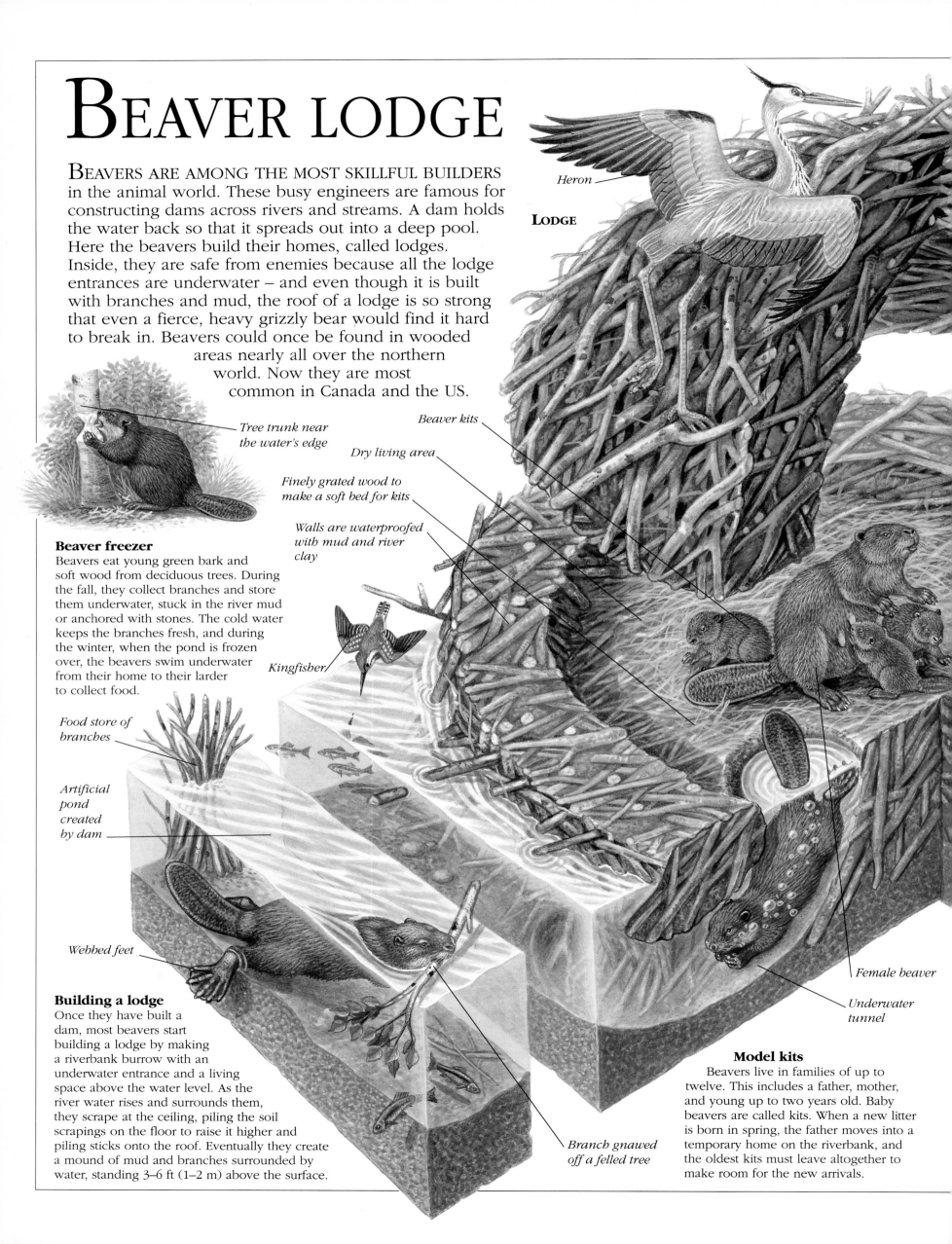

Heron

LODGE

Tree trunk near the water's edge

Beaver kits

Dry living area

Finely grated wood to make a soft bed for kits

Walls are waterproofed with mud and river clay

Beaver freezer

Beavers eat young green bark and soft wood from deciduous trees. During the fall, they collect branches and store them underwater, stuck in the river mud or anchored with stones. The cold water keeps the branches fresh, and during the winter, when the pond is frozen over, the beavers swim underwater from their home to their larder to collect food.

Kingfisher

Food store of branches

Artificial pond created by dam

Webbed feet

Female beaver

Underwater tunnel

Building a lodge

Once they have built a dam, most beavers start building a lodge by making a riverbank burrow with an underwater entrance and a living space above the water level. As the river water rises and surrounds them, they scrape at the ceiling, piling the soil scrapings on the floor to raise it higher and piling sticks onto the roof. Eventually they create a mound of mud and branches surrounded by water, standing 3–6 ft (1–2 m) above the surface.

Branch gnawed off a felled tree

Model kits

Beavers live in families of up to twelve. This includes a father, mother, and young up to two years old. Baby beavers are called kits. When a new litter is born in spring, the father moves into a temporary home on the riverbank, and the oldest kits must leave altogether to make room for the new arrivals.

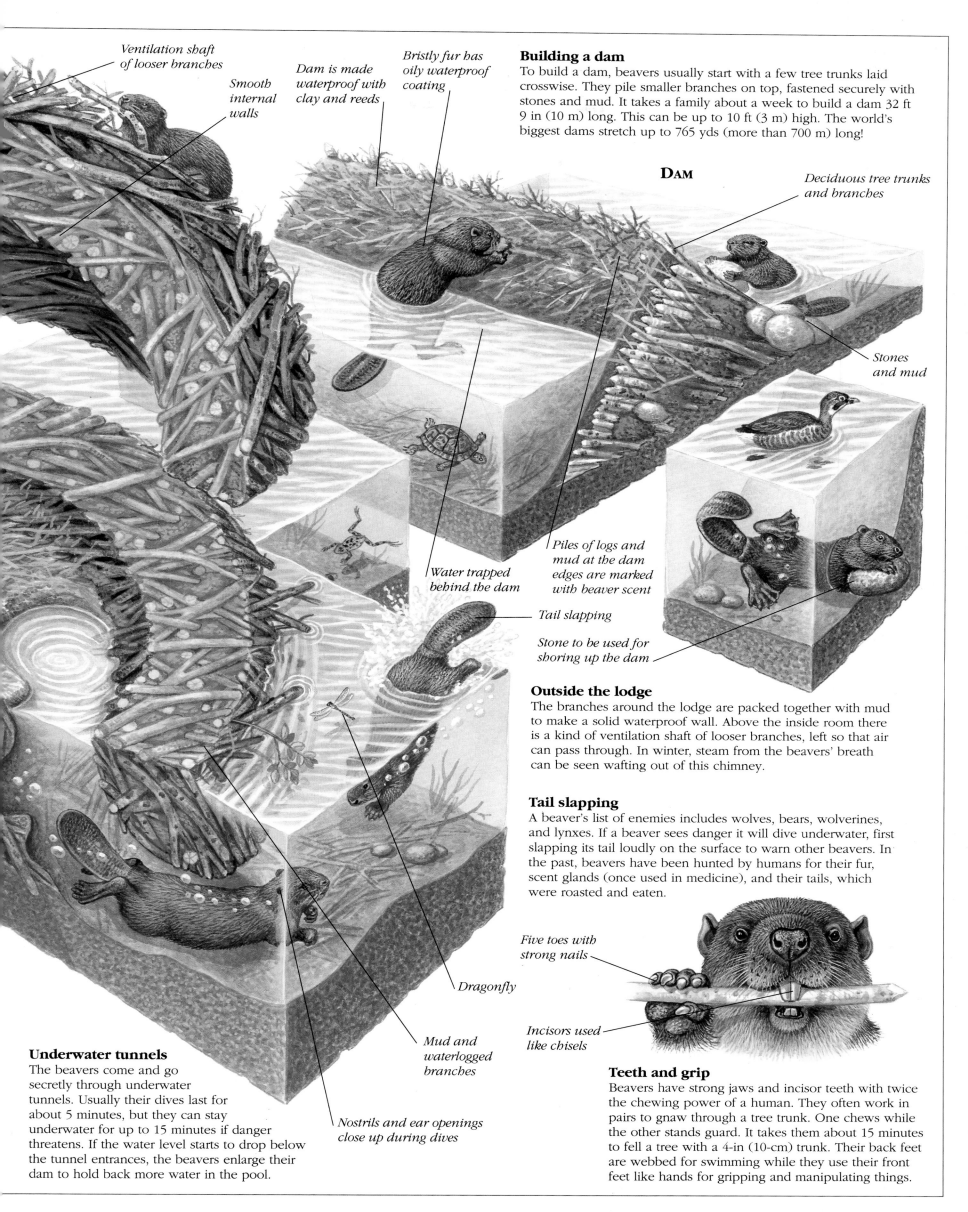

Ventilation shaft
of looser branches

Smooth
internal
walls

Dam is made
waterproof with
clay and reeds

Bristly fur has
oily waterproof
coating

Building a dam
To build a dam, beavers usually start with a few tree trunks laid crosswise. They pile smaller branches on top, fastened securely with stones and mud. It takes a family about a week to build a dam 32 ft 9 in (10 m) long. This can be up to 10 ft (3 m) high. The world's biggest dams stretch up to 765 yds (more than 700 m) long!

DAM

Deciduous tree trunks
and branches

Stones
and mud

Piles of logs and
mud at the dam
edges are marked
with beaver scent

Water trapped
behind the dam

Tail slapping

Stone to be used for
shoring up the dam

Outside the lodge
The branches around the lodge are packed together with mud to make a solid waterproof wall. Above the inside room there is a kind of ventilation shaft of looser branches, left so that air can pass through. In winter, steam from the beavers' breath can be seen wafting out of this chimney.

Tail slapping
A beaver's list of enemies includes wolves, bears, wolverines, and lynxes. If a beaver sees danger it will dive underwater, first slapping its tail loudly on the surface to warn other beavers. In the past, beavers have been hunted by humans for their fur, scent glands (once used in medicine), and their tails, which were roasted and eaten.

Five toes with
strong nails

Incisors used
like chisels

Dragonfly

Underwater tunnels
The beavers come and go secretly through underwater tunnels. Usually their dives last for about 5 minutes, but they can stay underwater for up to 15 minutes if danger threatens. If the water level starts to drop below the tunnel entrances, the beavers enlarge their dam to hold back more water in the pool.

Mud and
waterlogged
branches

Nostrils and ear openings
close up during dives

Teeth and grip
Beavers have strong jaws and incisor teeth with twice the chewing power of a human. They often work in pairs to gnaw through a tree trunk. One chews while the other stands guard. It takes them about 15 minutes to fell a tree with a 4-in (10-cm) trunk. Their back feet are webbed for swimming while they use their front feet like hands for gripping and manipulating things.

TERMITE CITY

IMAGINE STANDING IN THE BLAZING HEAT OF AN AFRICAN afternoon. After a while it would be difficult to withstand the searing hot rays of the sun. Yet one of the most numerous creatures that lives on the grasslands of Africa, a tiny insect called a termite, has skin so soft and thin that its internal organs show through to the outside. Termites survive the sun by avoiding it, sheltering inside one of the largest and most complex animal nests in nature. From the outside it looks like a towering fortress of baked mud. Inside there is a teeming insect city with up to two million termites busy at work. Secret underground tunnels lead to the outside world.

Building the fortress

Millions of termites work together to build a nest, called a termitarium. Each creature makes its own mini-bricks by chewing earth mixed with saliva. The tiny pellets are pushed onto the wall where they dry rock-hard. The biggest nests take decades to build. The largest stretch more than 26 ft (8 m) high.

Insect air-conditioning

Termites build tiny channels through the ribs of the nest and wider chimneys up the middle. During the day, the air inside warms up and rises through the chimneys. Then it travels down through the rib channels, passing near the outer surface and getting new supplies of oxygen.

Fungus gardening

Termites eat plant material. But the fibrous part of plants, called cellulose, is very difficult to digest. Worker termites collect leaf pieces and chew them up to make compost, which they use to fill chambers in the nest. To this mixture they add the spores of a unique type of fungus. Soon this grows into a thick mesh called a comb. It turns the compost into a crumbly mixture that the termites can eat.

TERMITE CASTES

In a termite nest, everything is highly organized. The termites are divided into different groups called castes. Each caste has a particular job to do. There are many species of termites. The examples shown below are from the African macrotermite group.

PRIMARY QUEEN
She never leaves the nest and grows to between 0.19 and 0.86 in (5 and 22 mm).

SECONDARY QUEEN
This substitute grows from the worker caste if the queen dies.

TERTIARY QUEEN
Another substitute that grows if something happens to the queen.

NASUTUS SOLDIER
A sterile female with a snout for shooting out gummy liquid. Her job is to guard the workers.

SOLDIER
Termite with sharp jaw parts (mandibles). It grows to between 0.11 and 0.78 in (3 and 20 mm).

PRIMARY KING
The king's only job is to fertilize the queen. Soon after they mate for the first time, both the king and the queen lose their wings.

WORKER
A sterile male or female. Workers do the building, foraging, cleaning, feeding, and nursery care in the nest.

LONG-WINGED NYMPH
A termite who will fly off to start a new colony.

Lilac-breasted rollers catch flying termites

Central chimney

Attic

Side chimney

Four-toed bedgehog forages for a meal

Mushroom provides spores for termites after it bas withered

Mongoose looks for insects in deserted mounds

Thick wall

African grassland, called savanna

Aardvark rips out part of nest

Strong claws for digging and ripping

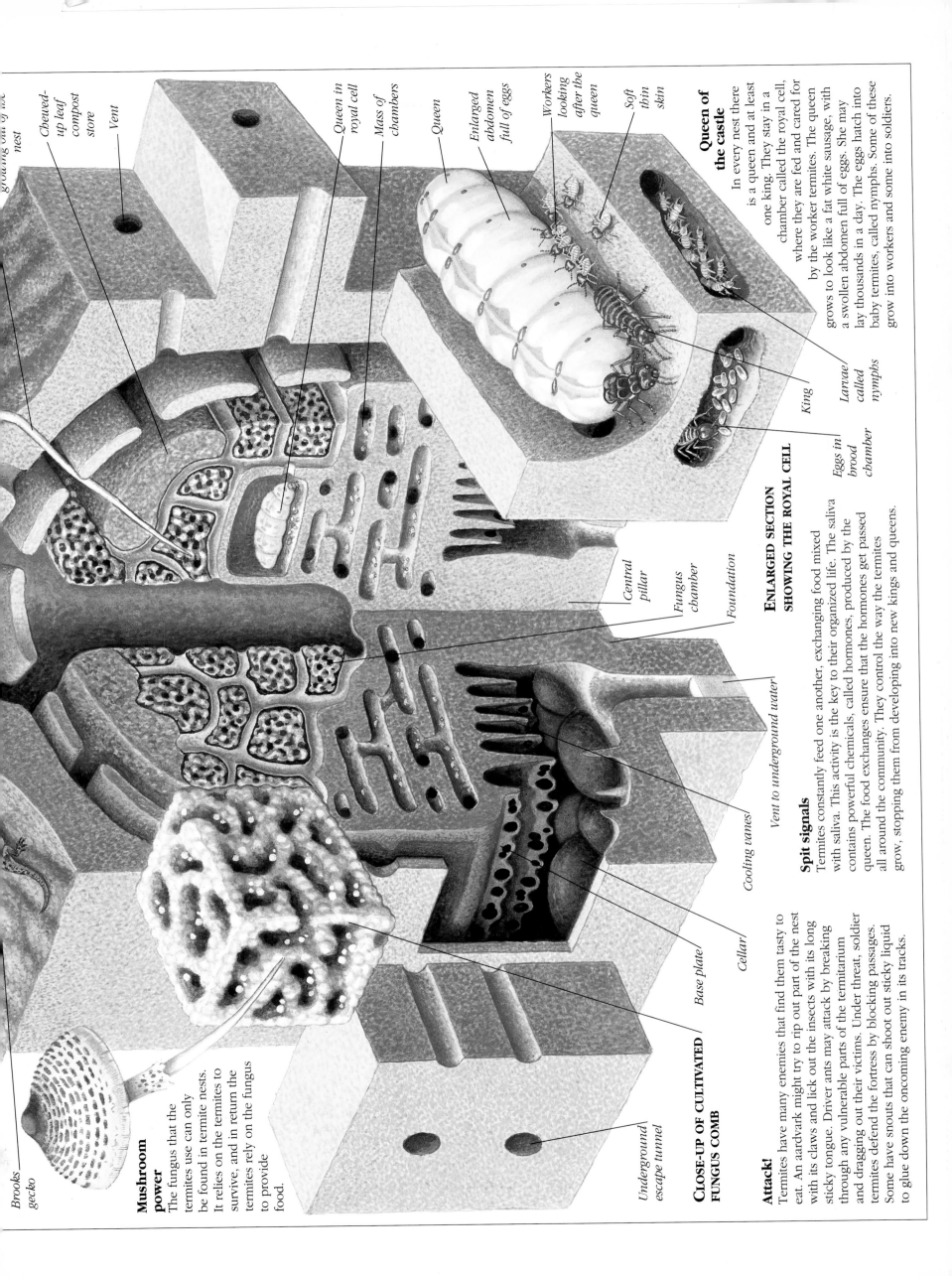

Growing out of the nest

Brooks gecko

Chewed-up leaf compost store

Vent

Mushroom power
The fungus that the termites use can only be found in termite nests. It relies on the termites to survive, and in return the termites rely on the fungus to provide food.

CLOSE-UP OF CULTIVATED FUNGUS COMB

Attack!
Termites have many enemies that find them tasty to eat. An aardvark might try to rip out part of the nest with its claws and lick out the insects with its long sticky tongue. Driver ants may attack by breaking through any vulnerable parts of the termitarium and dragging out their victims. Under threat, soldier termites defend the fortress by blocking passages. Some termites have snouts that can shoot out sticky liquid to glue down the oncoming enemy in its tracks.

Underground escape tunnel

Base plate

Cellar

Vent to underground water

Spit signals
Termites constantly feed one another, exchanging food mixed with saliva. This activity is the key to their organized life. The saliva contains powerful chemicals, called hormones, produced by the queen. The food exchanges ensure that the hormones get passed all around the community. They control the way the termites grow, stopping them from developing into new kings and queens.

Cooling vanes

Foundation

Fungus chamber

Central pillar

ENLARGED SECTION SHOWING THE ROYAL CELL

Eggs in brood chamber

Larvae called nymphs

King

Queen of the castle
In every nest there is a queen and at least one king. They stay in a chamber called the royal cell, where they are fed and cared for by the worker termites. The queen grows to look like a fat white sausage, with a swollen abdomen full of eggs. She may lay thousands in a day. The eggs hatch into baby termites, called nymphs. Some of these grow into workers and some into soldiers.

Soft thin skin

Workers looking after the queen

Enlarged abdomen full of eggs

Queen

Mass of chambers

Queen in royal cell

TROPICAL RIVERBANK

WATER IS THE LIFEBLOOD OF THE RAIN FORESTS around the Earth's equator. Streams and rivers flow through them, fed by daily rainfall. The greatest river is the Amazon, which begins as a stream high in the Andes Mountains. It travels 4,000 miles (6,400 km) east, emptying into the Atlantic Ocean. Its streams and tributaries wind through the world's biggest rain forest, where the cries of many creatures echo through the trees. Yet only ripples and the odd splash made by a jumping fish give any clue to the abundance of life beneath the water surface. In fact there are some 1,500 known types of Amazon fish, and probably more than 1,000 yet to be discovered! This vast flowing water network is one of the biggest and most mysterious wildlife homes on our planet.

Bald bats
The Amazon is home to the strange fish-eating bat. This species is almost hairless, with long narrow wings and sharp claws. Swooping low over the water, the bats impale fish on their claws and fly away to their roosts.

Amazon kingfisher

Fish-eating bat

Amazonian manatee

Gentle giants
Manatees are large, timid, nearsighted mammals. They spend their time grazing on underwater plants, which they rip at with a strong, large upper lip, only surfacing when they need to breathe. They communicate with each other by muzzle-to-muzzle touching and by making a chirping sound when they are alarmed.

Amazonian giant otter

River dolphin

Striped headstander

Clever clickers
Amazon river dolphins live in pairs and are freshwater animals only found in the Amazon. To navigate and hunt in the murky water they use echolocation. They make a series of clicks in their air passages and when the sounds strike an object, the dolphins pick up the rebounding echos, which they use to judge the distance and direction of the object.

Neon tetra

Prochilodus insignis

Marbled hatchet fish

Arapaima fish

Layered life
Fish are adapted to live in different parts of the river. The catfish is a bottom-dweller. It has a flattened underside so it can hug the riverbed as it searches for food. Mid-water tetra fish are constantly on the move, so they are small, streamlined, and agile. The arawana is a surface feeder, so it is slim, enabling it to hold a steady position in the current.

Surubim

Banded knife fish

Discus fish

Electric eel

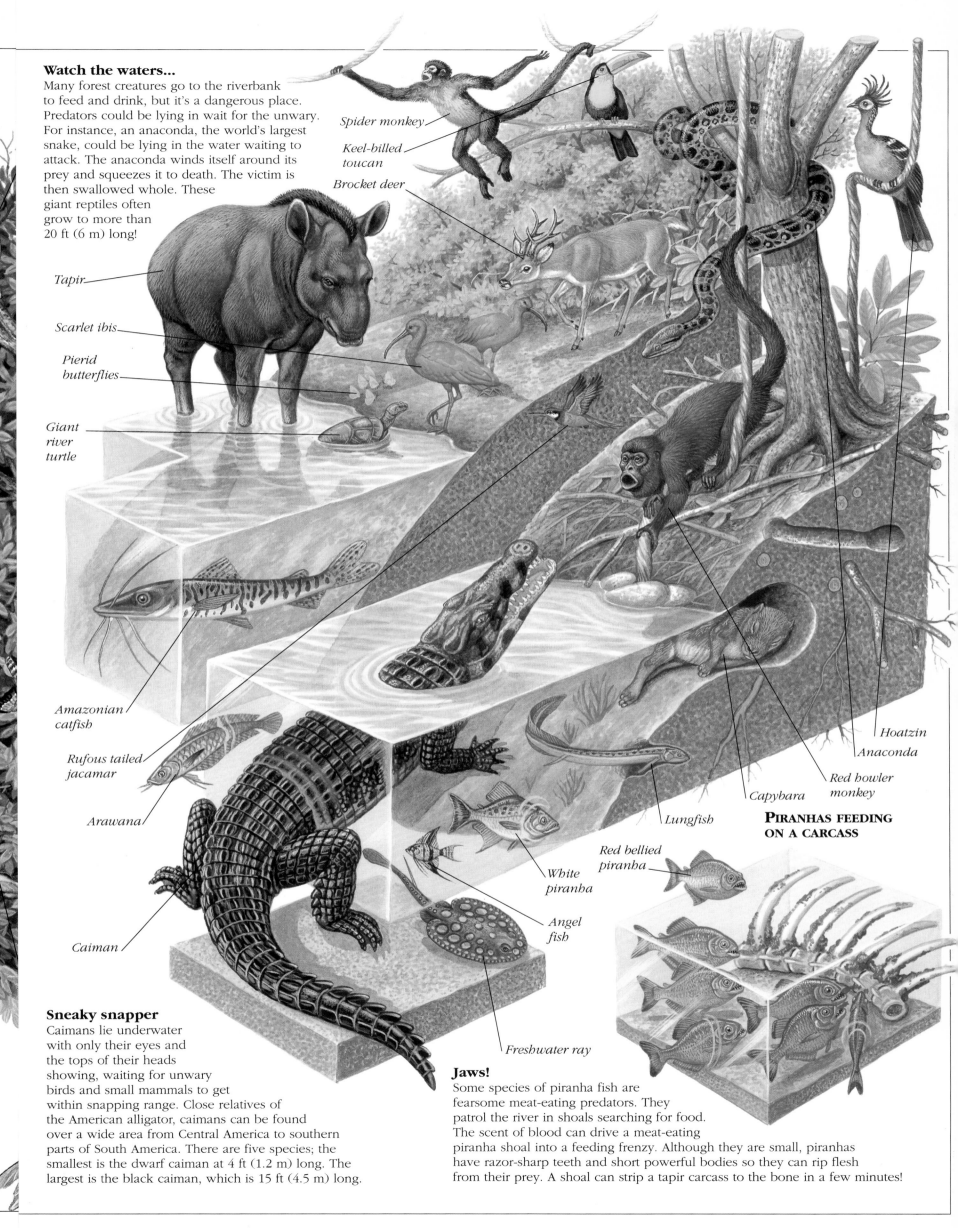

Watch the waters...
Many forest creatures go to the riverbank to feed and drink, but it's a dangerous place. Predators could be lying in wait for the unwary. For instance, an anaconda, the world's largest snake, could be lying in the water waiting to attack. The anaconda winds itself around its prey and squeezes it to death. The victim is then swallowed whole. These giant reptiles often grow to more than 20 ft (6 m) long!

Spider monkey

Keel-billed toucan

Brocket deer

Tapir

Scarlet ibis

Pierid butterflies

Giant river turtle

Amazonian catfish

Rufous tailed jacamar

Arawana

Caiman

Hoatzin

Anaconda

Red howler monkey

Capybara

Lungfish

PIRANHAS FEEDING ON A CARCASS

White piranha

Red bellied piranha

Angel fish

Freshwater ray

Sneaky snapper
Caimans lie underwater with only their eyes and the tops of their heads showing, waiting for unwary birds and small mammals to get within snapping range. Close relatives of the American alligator, caimans can be found over a wide area from Central America to southern parts of South America. There are five species; the smallest is the dwarf caiman at 4 ft (1.2 m) long. The largest is the black caiman, which is 15 ft (4.5 m) long.

Jaws!
Some species of piranha fish are fearsome meat-eating predators. They patrol the river in shoals searching for food. The scent of blood can drive a meat-eating piranha shoal into a feeding frenzy. Although they are small, piranhas have razor-sharp teeth and short powerful bodies so they can rip flesh from their prey. A shoal can strip a tapir carcass to the bone in a few minutes!

WOODLAND

IF YOU TAKE A WALK THROUGH A FOREST IN A NORTHERN part of the world, it might seem to be a calm, peaceful place. But unseen, and perhaps very close to you, a life-and-death battle might be taking place, animals might be busy building homes and giving birth, or a stealthy hunter might be stalking its prey. Large areas of deciduous woodland flourish in North America, Europe, and central Asia, where there is mild weather and regular rainfall. Deciduous woodlands contain broad-leaved trees that drop all their leaves seasonally every winter. Oak, elm, and beech trees are all deciduous. This picture shows a European deciduous woodland – home to a large variety of plants and animals.

European brown bear

Crow

Great tit

Sparrowhawk

Fallow deer with fawn

Foxes in their burrow, called an earth

Big bears
The woodland animal that strikes most fear into humans is the bear. The European brown bear in this picture can weigh up to 550 lb (250 kg) and reach 8 ft (2.5 m) high standing on its hind legs. Although female bears can be particularly dangerous when defending their cubs, bears are normally shy creatures. In fact, they are very nearsighted. They make up for it with a sharp sense of hearing and of smell.

Mole

Bird land
Insects, nuts, seeds, and berries make the woods a rich summer feeding ground for birds. Their bodies are adapted to help them feed in different ways. Woodpeckers have stiff tails and feet with toes to help them cling to tree trunks. Their pointed beaks are good for digging into trunks, and their long tongues reach insects under the bark.

LEAF LITTER

Drassodes spider

Sexton beetle

Great brown weevil larva

Litter bugs
Insects make up 70 percent of the animal species in a woodland. Some insects live in the layer of dead leaves known as leaf litter. Together with fungi and bacteria, they break down the dead leaves. This material is then churned up by earthworms that mix the nutrients from the leaves with the soil, making it rich enough for new plants to grow in. The whole process takes about two years.

Worm cast

Centipede

Bank vole

Jay with an acorn

Earthworm

Sow bug

Wireworm

The twilight zone
Foxes, badgers, moles, and rabbits are just some of the animals that make their homes underground. The mole is highly suited to this lifestyle. On the end of its short, wide front legs are claws that turn outward, which are ideal for digging and crawling. Because they spend most of their life in the dark, moles are very nearsighted

Sulphur butterfly

European hedgehog

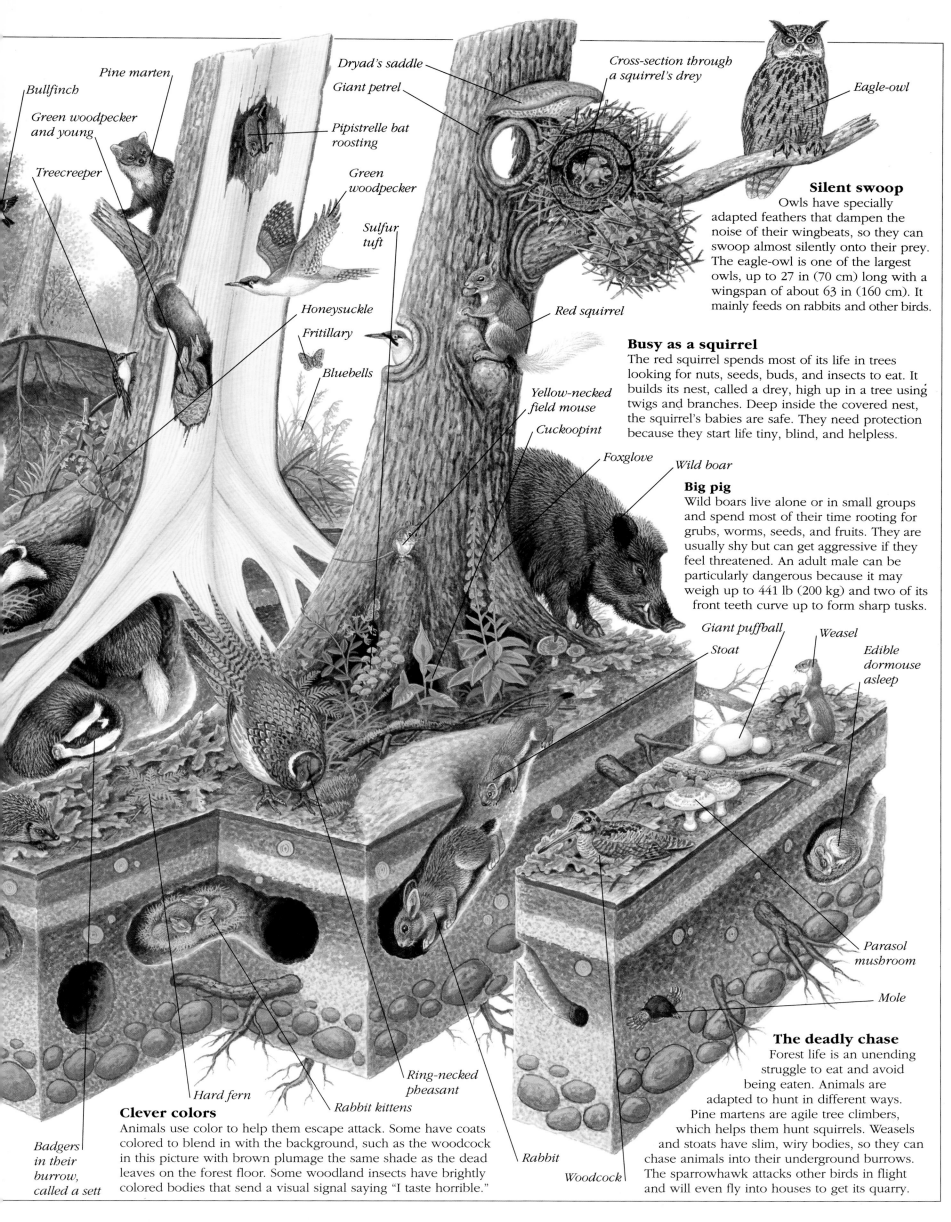

Bullfinch

Pine marten

Green woodpecker and young

Treecreeper

Dryad's saddle

Giant petrel

Pipistrelle bat roosting

Green woodpecker

Sulfur tuft

Honeysuckle

Fritillary

Bluebells

Cross-section through a squirrel's drey

Eagle-owl

Red squirrel

Yellow-necked field mouse

Cuckoopint

Foxglove

Wild boar

Silent swoop
Owls have specially adapted feathers that dampen the noise of their wingbeats, so they can swoop almost silently onto their prey. The eagle-owl is one of the largest owls, up to 27 in (70 cm) long with a wingspan of about 63 in (160 cm). It mainly feeds on rabbits and other birds.

Busy as a squirrel
The red squirrel spends most of its life in trees looking for nuts, seeds, buds, and insects to eat. It builds its nest, called a drey, high up in a tree using twigs and branches. Deep inside the covered nest, the squirrel's babies are safe. They need protection because they start life tiny, blind, and helpless.

Big pig
Wild boars live alone or in small groups and spend most of their time rooting for grubs, worms, seeds, and fruits. They are usually shy but can get aggressive if they feel threatened. An adult male can be particularly dangerous because it may weigh up to 441 lb (200 kg) and two of its front teeth curve up to form sharp tusks.

Giant puffball

Stoat

Weasel

Edible dormouse asleep

Parasol mushroom

Mole

Hard fern

Rabbit kittens

Ring-necked pheasant

Badgers in their burrow, called a sett

Rabbit

Woodcock

Clever colors
Animals use color to help them escape attack. Some have coats colored to blend in with the background, such as the woodcock in this picture with brown plumage the same shade as the dead leaves on the forest floor. Some woodland insects have brightly colored bodies that send a visual signal saying "I taste horrible."

The deadly chase
Forest life is an unending struggle to eat and avoid being eaten. Animals are adapted to hunt in different ways. Pine martens are agile tree climbers, which helps them hunt squirrels. Weasels and stoats have slim, wiry bodies, so they can chase animals into their underground burrows. The sparrowhawk attacks other birds in flight and will even fly into houses to get its quarry.

OAK TREE

THIS TALL, MAJESTIC OAK TREE MAY HAVE lived for up to 600 years, spreading its branches up to 100 ft (30 m) high.

Oak wood is prized for its strength and has been used for centuries to build palaces and galleons, treasure chests and thrones. Yet an oak starts life as a tiny acorn no bigger than a thumbnail, and it has to survive many dangers. Insects, birds, and squirrels eat acorns, and even if one takes root, it may still be eaten or stepped on. These mighty giants of the forest have a tough childhood!

Foliage feeders

Oak leaves provide food for insects. A big oak can support up to 400,000 caterpillars at once. It defends itself from insect attacks by quickly replacing eaten buds and producing a bitter chemical, called tannin, that repels insects.

Food-making leaves

Leaves make nutrients (the tree's food) using a green chemical called chlorophyll. In sunlight, each leaf photosynthesizes. This means that the chlorophyll traps energy from sunlight and uses it to convert minerals and water (brought up from the tree roots) and air (taken in through tiny holes called stomata in the leaves) into food.

Oak galls

Many oak trees have wartlike growths on them called galls. They are caused when insects lay their eggs somewhere on the oak and secrete substances that make tree cells grow around the eggs. This helps both the insect and the tree. The gall surrounds the larva (growing insect) so that it can't attack the rest of the tree, while the larva gets food and shelter inside the gall. Birds peck at galls to get at the larva inside.

OAK GALLS

Marble gall

Oak-apple gall

Gall wasp

Common spangle gall

Gall wasps

There are many types of galls. The oak-apple gall is one of the most common. It is caused by a wasp that lays its eggs in leaf buds in spring. The oak-apple gall grows around the eggs.

Jay

Stock dove

Redstart

Wryneck

Chaffinch

Blackcap

Rook

Red kite

Turtle dove

Golden oriole

Song thrush

Magpie

Blue tit

Pied flycatcher

All about bark
The bark is the rough outer layer of a tree. It helps prevent damage from animals, stops the tree from drying out, and protects it from heat and cold. As the tree grows thicker, its bark stretches and splits.

Tawny owl

Oak bark beetle

Gallery made by oak bark beetle

Sulfur tuft fungi

Garlic snail

Stag beetle larva

Slug

Blusher

Mole

Rooting around
In spring and summer, the roots suck up water and minerals to help produce the tree's food. In fall and winter, any unused food is carried back down to the roots to be stored underground until the spring. The roots also support the tree; oak roots are particularly strong, so oaks withstand centuries of storms and high winds.

Great spotted woodpecker

Lynx

Stag beetle

Song thrush

From the acorn
Acorns are the fruit of the oak tree. Each acorn grows in a cup attached to a twig. The hard acorn shell protects the soft seed inside. Only one in a million acorns makes it to the tree stage. The rest are eaten by animals such as insects, squirrels, and jays. In the Middle Ages, farmers took their pigs into the forest to graze on fallen acorns.

Tree killers
Fungi are plants, but they do not contain chlorophyll and so cannot make food by photosynthesis. They take their food from decaying or living things, including oaks. Spindleshank fungus, shown above, anchors itself to an oak's trunk. Fungi are spread by tiny seeds called spores.

Yellow-necked field mouse

Spindleshank fungus

Gray squirrel

Nuthatch

Starling

Wood warbler

Purple emperor

Polecat

Common shrew

Dryad's saddle

Wood pigeons and nest

Birth of a tree
Stage 1:
In spring, the seed inside a fallen acorn sends a root down into the soil. The root sucks up water and minerals. **Stage 2:** The seed sends up a shoot into the light and two rounded seed leaves open out to reveal a tiny bud. **Stage 3:** As the first proper tree leaves grow, the roots lengthen to find more nutrients. In autumn, the leaves fall, leaving a new bud that will start to grow in the spring.

BIRTH OF A TREE

Acorn

1 2 3

Root gall

ANTARCTIC LIFE

ANTARCTICA IS A HUGE CONTINENT THE SIZE OF THE US and South America combined. It is the southernmost land on Earth – a barren, dangerous world permanently covered by thick ice and surrounded by the stormy Antarctic Ocean. It lies in darkness for six months of the year and during these bleak winter months, half of the ocean freezes over and temperatures on the mainland fall to -94° F (-70° C). In this climate very few animals can survive, but when the sun returns in September, the ocean begins to melt around the edges of the land. Lots of animals arrive to breed on the shores before the harsh snowstorms of winter return in February.

Flabby fighters

During the summer, more than 300,000 elephant seals arrive to breed on the Antarctic island of South Georgia. The crowded beaches become noisy, dangerous places as the giant males rear up to fight each other for females. They roar out challenges and crash into each other, biting ferociously.

Colonies and crabeaters

Many millions of seals breed in groups called colonies around the edge of Antarctica. Species include Weddell seals, Ross seals, and crabeater seals. There are thought to be as many as thirty million crabeaters, making them by far the largest group. They spend most of their lives in the water or hauled up on floating ice blocks called floes. They look clumsy on land, but in the water they are graceful, acrobatic swimmers.

Baby stealers

Skuas are large seabirds with sharp, hooked beaks. They nest near penguin colonies so they can steal chicks and eggs to eat. They even attack small birds in the air, carrying on daring acrobatic chases until they force their victims to regurgitate the food they have eaten. Small petrels travel to and from their nests under cover of darkness to avoid these vicious airborne pirates.

Antifreeze fish

In winter, when the sea surface has turned to ice, life continues in the icy waters below. Antarctic fish have adapted to survive the cold – most of them have a kind of antifreeze in their bodies that keeps their blood from freezing up.

Sinister smilers

Leopard seals are well named – just like leopards, they are cunning predators. Along with krill and fish, they like to eat penguins, and even human divers are not safe from their attack. Their upturned mouths give them a sinister-looking smile, concealing ferocious teeth. They will sometimes smash up through a layer of ice to snatch an unsuspecting penguin walking above.

Counting krill

Krill are small shrimplike creatures about 2 in (5 cm) long. There are an estimated 590 million tons (600 million tonnes) of them altogether. Krill are vital for the survival of the animals that visit Antarctica to breed. In winter they settle underneath the pack ice to eat algae. In summer they swim together in giant swarms, providing a feast for whales, seals, and penguins.

Gentoo penguin

Elephant seal

Antarctic skua

Crabeater seal

Chinstrap penguin

Dove prion

Ice fish

Snow petrel

Toothfish

Antarctic cod

Krill

Leopard seal

White-headed petrel

Great-winged petrel

Cape pigeon

White-chinned petrel

Blue petrel

Young Ross seal

Killer whale

Killer gangs

There are two groups of whales in the Antarctic Ocean. Baleen whales eat krill, sifting it through bony plates in their mouths. Toothed whales hunt for larger prey. Among this group are the fast and ferocious killer whales. They hunt in gangs called pods, working cleverly together to trap seals and other small whales. They have even been known to chase human explorers.

King penguin

Blue-eyed shag

Ross seal

Emperor penguin and chick

Emperor penguins

Emperor penguins breed at a different time from all the other Antarctic animals. Each female lays one egg in the fall. She transfers it to the male, who keeps it warm in a pouch above his feet. The males gather together in a huddle while the females go off to the ocean to feed. During this time, the males stand in darkness, without food, enduring the fiercest, coldest winter storms anywhere in the world.

Adelie penguins

Adelies are the most common Antarctic penguins. They breed in large colonies and, like other penguins, one parent stays sitting on the egg while the other goes to the ocean to feed. When the chicks are three weeks old, they waddle over to join nearby "creches," or huddles of other chicks. These babies stay together to keep warm and safe while both parents go off to find food. When a parent returns, it can recognize its own chick's call.

Adelie penguin

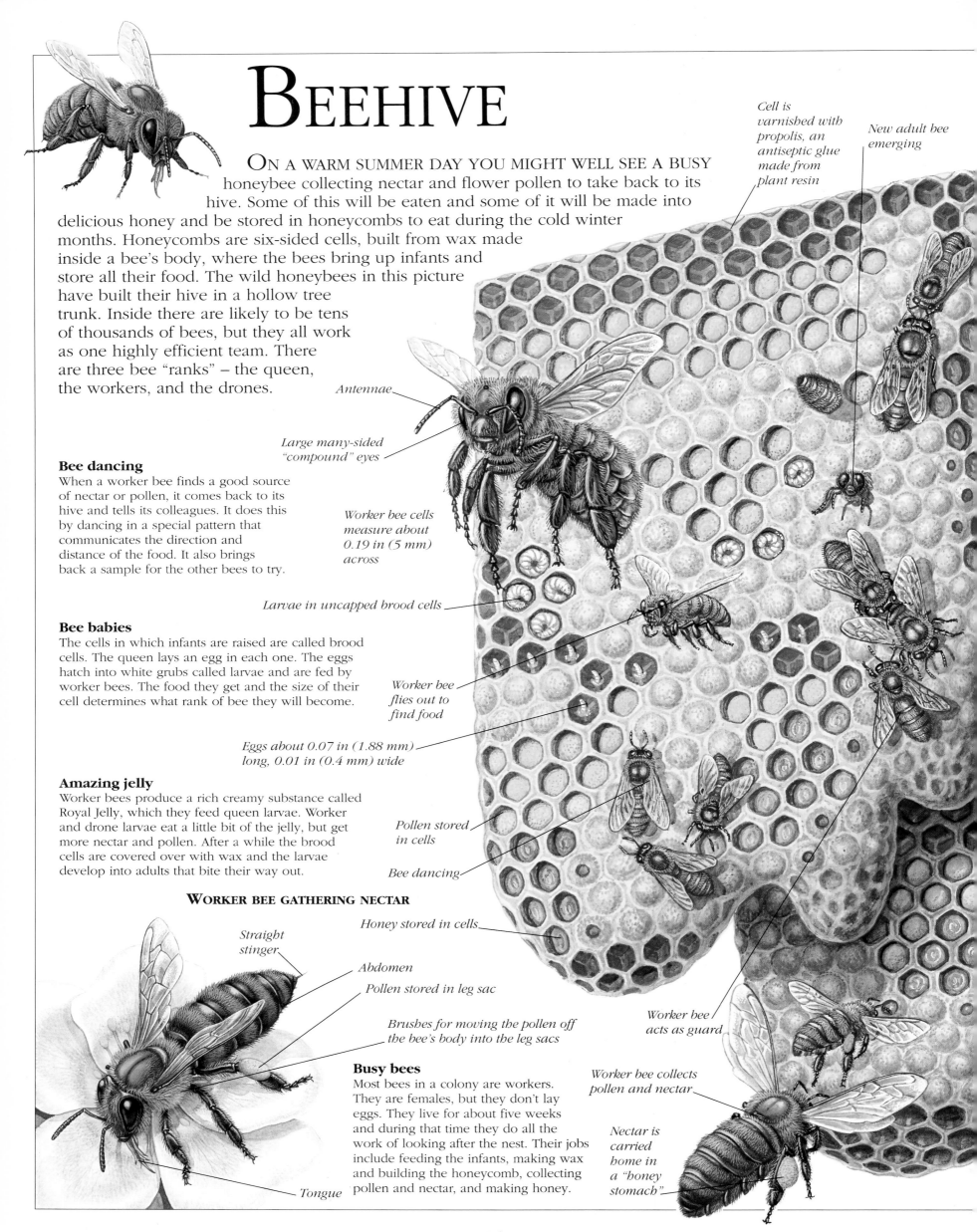

BEEHIVE

ON A WARM SUMMER DAY YOU MIGHT WELL SEE A BUSY honeybee collecting nectar and flower pollen to take back to its hive. Some of this will be eaten and some of it will be made into delicious honey and be stored in honeycombs to eat during the cold winter months. Honeycombs are six-sided cells, built from wax made inside a bee's body, where the bees bring up infants and store all their food. The wild honeybees in this picture have built their hive in a hollow tree trunk. Inside there are likely to be tens of thousands of bees, but they all work as one highly efficient team. There are three bee "ranks" – the queen, the workers, and the drones.

Cell is varnished with propolis, an antiseptic glue made from plant resin

New adult bee emerging

Bee dancing

When a worker bee finds a good source of nectar or pollen, it comes back to its hive and tells its colleagues. It does this by dancing in a special pattern that communicates the direction and distance of the food. It also brings back a sample for the other bees to try.

Bee babies

The cells in which infants are raised are called brood cells. The queen lays an egg in each one. The eggs hatch into white grubs called larvae and are fed by worker bees. The food they get and the size of their cell determines what rank of bee they will become.

Amazing jelly

Worker bees produce a rich creamy substance called Royal Jelly, which they feed queen larvae. Worker and drone larvae eat a little bit of the jelly, but get more nectar and pollen. After a while the brood cells are covered over with wax and the larvae develop into adults that bite their way out.

Antennae

Large many-sided "compound" eyes

Worker bee cells measure about 0.19 in (5 mm) across

Larvae in uncapped brood cells

Worker bee flies out to find food

Eggs about 0.07 in (1.88 mm) long, 0.01 in (0.4 mm) wide

Pollen stored in cells

Bee dancing

WORKER BEE GATHERING NECTAR

Honey stored in cells

Straight stinger

Abdomen

Pollen stored in leg sac

Brushes for moving the pollen off the bee's body into the leg sacs

Busy bees

Most bees in a colony are workers. They are females, but they don't lay eggs. They live for about five weeks and during that time they do all the work of looking after the nest. Their jobs include feeding the infants, making wax and building the honeycomb, collecting pollen and nectar, and making honey.

Tongue

Worker bee acts as guard

Worker bee collects pollen and nectar

Nectar is carried home in a "honey stomach"

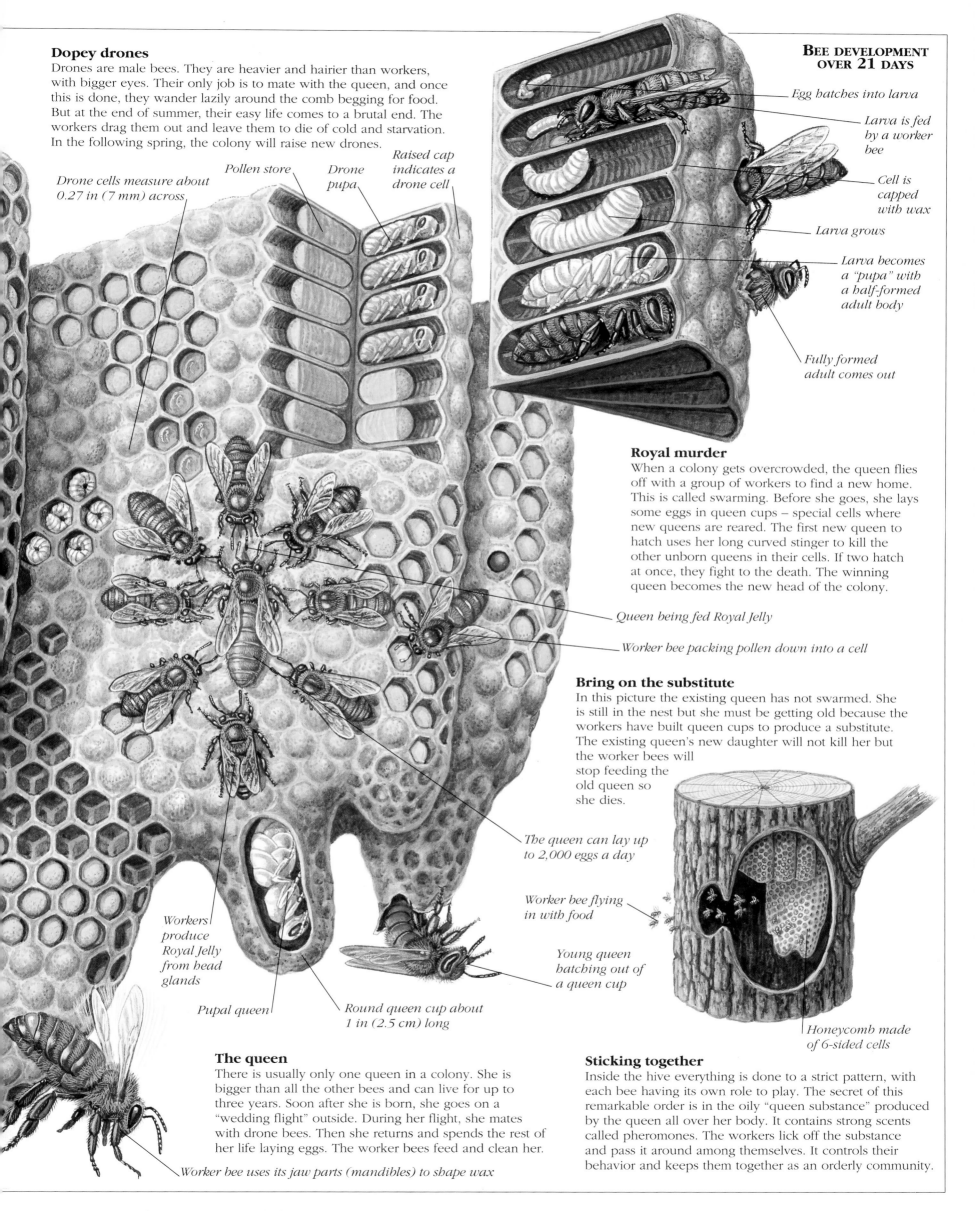

Dopey drones

Drones are male bees. They are heavier and hairier than workers, with bigger eyes. Their only job is to mate with the queen, and once this is done, they wander lazily around the comb begging for food. But at the end of summer, their easy life comes to a brutal end. The workers drag them out and leave them to die of cold and starvation. In the following spring, the colony will raise new drones.

Drone cells measure about 0.27 in (7 mm) across

Pollen store

Drone pupa

Raised cap indicates a drone cell

Egg hatches into larva

Larva is fed by a worker bee

Cell is capped with wax

Larva grows

Larva becomes a "pupa" with a half-formed adult body

Fully formed adult comes out

Royal murder

When a colony gets overcrowded, the queen flies off with a group of workers to find a new home. This is called swarming. Before she goes, she lays some eggs in queen cups – special cells where new queens are reared. The first new queen to hatch uses her long curved stinger to kill the other unborn queens in their cells. If two hatch at once, they fight to the death. The winning queen becomes the new head of the colony.

Queen being fed Royal Jelly

Worker bee packing pollen down into a cell

Bring on the substitute

In this picture the existing queen has not swarmed. She is still in the nest but she must be getting old because the workers have built queen cups to produce a substitute. The existing queen's new daughter will not kill her but the worker bees will stop feeding the old queen so she dies.

The queen can lay up to 2,000 eggs a day

Worker bee flying in with food

Young queen hatching out of a queen cup

Workers produce Royal Jelly from head glands

Pupal queen

Round queen cup about 1 in (2.5 cm) long

Honeycomb made of 6-sided cells

The queen

There is usually only one queen in a colony. She is bigger than all the other bees and can live for up to three years. Soon after she is born, she goes on a "wedding flight" outside. During her flight, she mates with drone bees. Then she returns and spends the rest of her life laying eggs. The worker bees feed and clean her.

Worker bee uses its jaw parts (mandibles) to shape wax

Sticking together

Inside the hive everything is done to a strict pattern, with each bee having its own role to play. The secret of this remarkable order is in the oily "queen substance" produced by the queen all over her body. It contains strong scents called pheromones. The workers lick off the substance and pass it around among themselves. It controls their behavior and keeps them together as an orderly community.

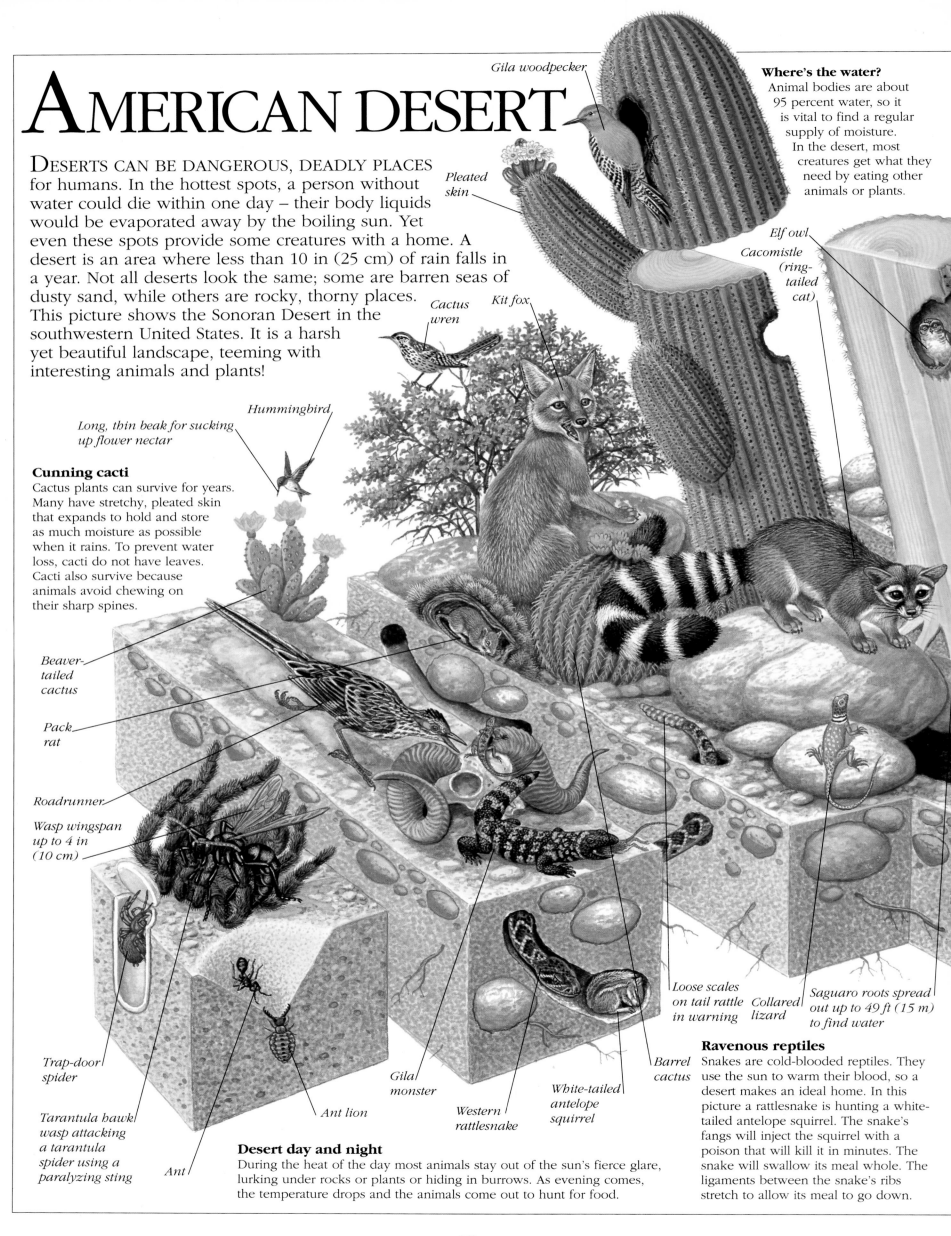

AMERICAN DESERT

DESERTS CAN BE DANGEROUS, DEADLY PLACES for humans. In the hottest spots, a person without water could die within one day – their body liquids would be evaporated away by the boiling sun. Yet even these spots provide some creatures with a home. A desert is an area where less than 10 in (25 cm) of rain falls in a year. Not all deserts look the same; some are barren seas of dusty sand, while others are rocky, thorny places. This picture shows the Sonoran Desert in the southwestern United States. It is a harsh yet beautiful landscape, teeming with interesting animals and plants!

Gila woodpecker

Pleated skin

Where's the water?
Animal bodies are about 95 percent water, so it is vital to find a regular supply of moisture. In the desert, most creatures get what they need by eating other animals or plants.

Elf owl

Cacomistle (ring-tailed cat)

Cactus wren

Kit fox

Hummingbird

Long, thin beak for sucking up flower nectar

Cunning cacti
Cactus plants can survive for years. Many have stretchy, pleated skin that expands to hold and store as much moisture as possible when it rains. To prevent water loss, cacti do not have leaves. Cacti also survive because animals avoid chewing on their sharp spines.

Beaver-tailed cactus

Pack rat

Roadrunner

Wasp wingspan up to 4 in (10 cm)

Trap-door spider

Tarantula hawk wasp attacking a tarantula spider using a paralyzing sting

Ant

Ant lion

Gila monster

Desert day and night
During the heat of the day most animals stay out of the sun's fierce glare, lurking under rocks or plants or hiding in burrows. As evening comes, the temperature drops and the animals come out to hunt for food.

Western rattlesnake

White-tailed antelope squirrel

Loose scales on tail rattle in warning

Collared lizard

Saguaro roots spread out up to 49 ft (15 m) to find water

Barrel cactus

Ravenous reptiles
Snakes are cold-blooded reptiles. They use the sun to warm their blood, so a desert makes an ideal home. In this picture a rattlesnake is hunting a white-tailed antelope squirrel. The snake's fangs will inject the squirrel with a poison that will kill it in minutes. The snake will swallow its meal whole. The ligaments between the snake's ribs stretch to allow its meal to go down.

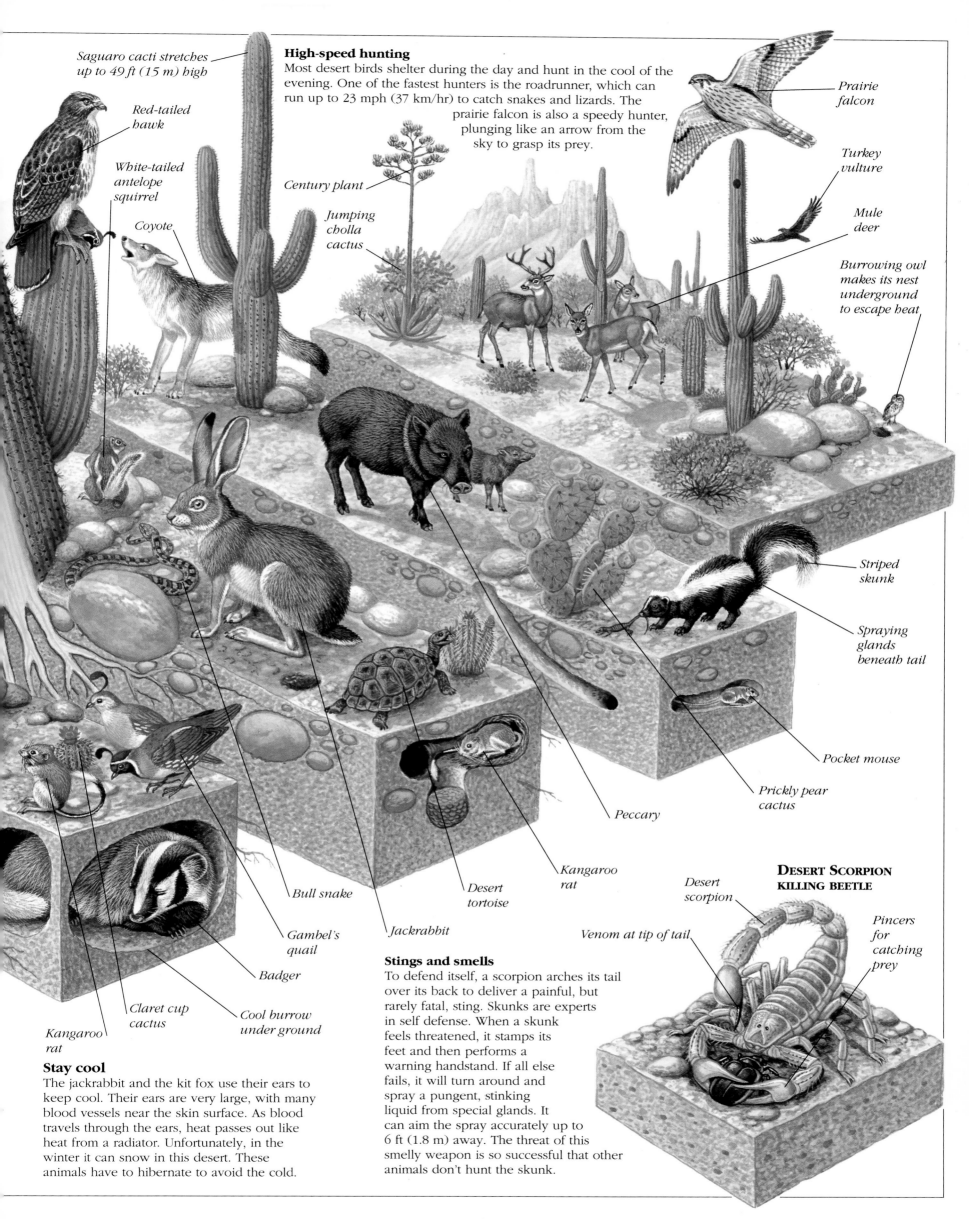

Saguaro cacti stretches up to 49 ft (15 m) high

Red-tailed hawk

White-tailed antelope squirrel

Coyote

High-speed hunting
Most desert birds shelter during the day and hunt in the cool of the evening. One of the fastest hunters is the roadrunner, which can run up to 23 mph (37 km/hr) to catch snakes and lizards. The prairie falcon is also a speedy hunter, plunging like an arrow from the sky to grasp its prey.

Prairie falcon

Turkey vulture

Mule deer

Burrowing owl makes its nest underground to escape heat

Century plant

Jumping cholla cactus

Striped skunk

Spraying glands beneath tail

Pocket mouse

Prickly pear cactus

Peccary

Kangaroo rat

Desert tortoise

Bull snake

Jackrabbit

Gambel's quail

Badger

Claret cup cactus

Cool burrow under ground

Kangaroo rat

Stay cool
The jackrabbit and the kit fox use their ears to keep cool. Their ears are very large, with many blood vessels near the skin surface. As blood travels through the ears, heat passes out like heat from a radiator. Unfortunately, in the winter it can snow in this desert. These animals have to hibernate to avoid the cold.

Stings and smells
To defend itself, a scorpion arches its tail over its back to deliver a painful, but rarely fatal, sting. Skunks are experts in self defense. When a skunk feels threatened, it stamps its feet and then performs a warning handstand. If all else fails, it will turn around and spray a pungent, stinking liquid from special glands. It can aim the spray accurately up to 6 ft (1.8 m) away. The threat of this smelly weapon is so successful that other animals don't hunt the skunk.

DESERT SCORPION
KILLING BEETLE

Desert scorpion

Venom at tip of tail

Pincers for catching prey

OCEAN

PHOTOGRAPHS OF THE EARTH TAKEN FROM OUTER SPACE LOOK MOSTLY blue. About 70 percent of the Earth's surface is covered by ocean, so the blue color is the water. If you dove beneath the waves, you would find an amazing watery world where creatures of all shapes and sizes make their homes, from giant ferocious sharks to tiny floating animals too small for humans to see. Sea life varies depending on the depth and temperature of the water. This picture shows some of the animals to be found in the Pacific Ocean.

Snacks for sea birds
Sea birds gather wherever there is food near the water's surface. Some of them dive for fish; others float on top of the waves spearing fish with their beaks. Some are even pirates, stealing food from other birds. They all have oil-covered feathers that keep them waterproof. Most sea birds live close to the coast, but a few spend many months far out at sea.

You're lunch!
In the sea, tiny fish are eaten by small fish, which are then eaten by large fish. This is known as a food chain. At the beginning of the ocean food chain there are tiny floating plants called phytoplankton, found near the sea's surface. They are eaten by microscopic creatures called zooplankton.

Danger at the top
On the surface floats a Portuguese man o'war. Its poisonous tentacles kill any fish that swims too near.

EPIPELAGIC ZONE

CROSS-SECTION THROUGH CORAL

All about corals
Corals need warm water and sunlight, so they are found where the seabed is near the surface. Corals are made up of many tiny animals called polyps. Each polyp has a ring of tentacles that it uses to sieve particles of food from the water around it. Some corals are hard and some are soft. Each hard coral polyp grows a limestone case to protect itself.

Laysan albatross

Frigate birds

Blue-footed booby

Sailfish

Flying fish

Portuguese man o'war

Hammerhead shark

Powder blue surgeon fish

Blue angel fish

Common dolphin

Ling cod

Barred surf perch

Snapper

Manta ray

Pacific barracuda

Pacific sardine

Eastern little tuna

Spotted moray eel

Sheepshead

Unicorn-fish

Four saddle puffer

Ocean sunfish

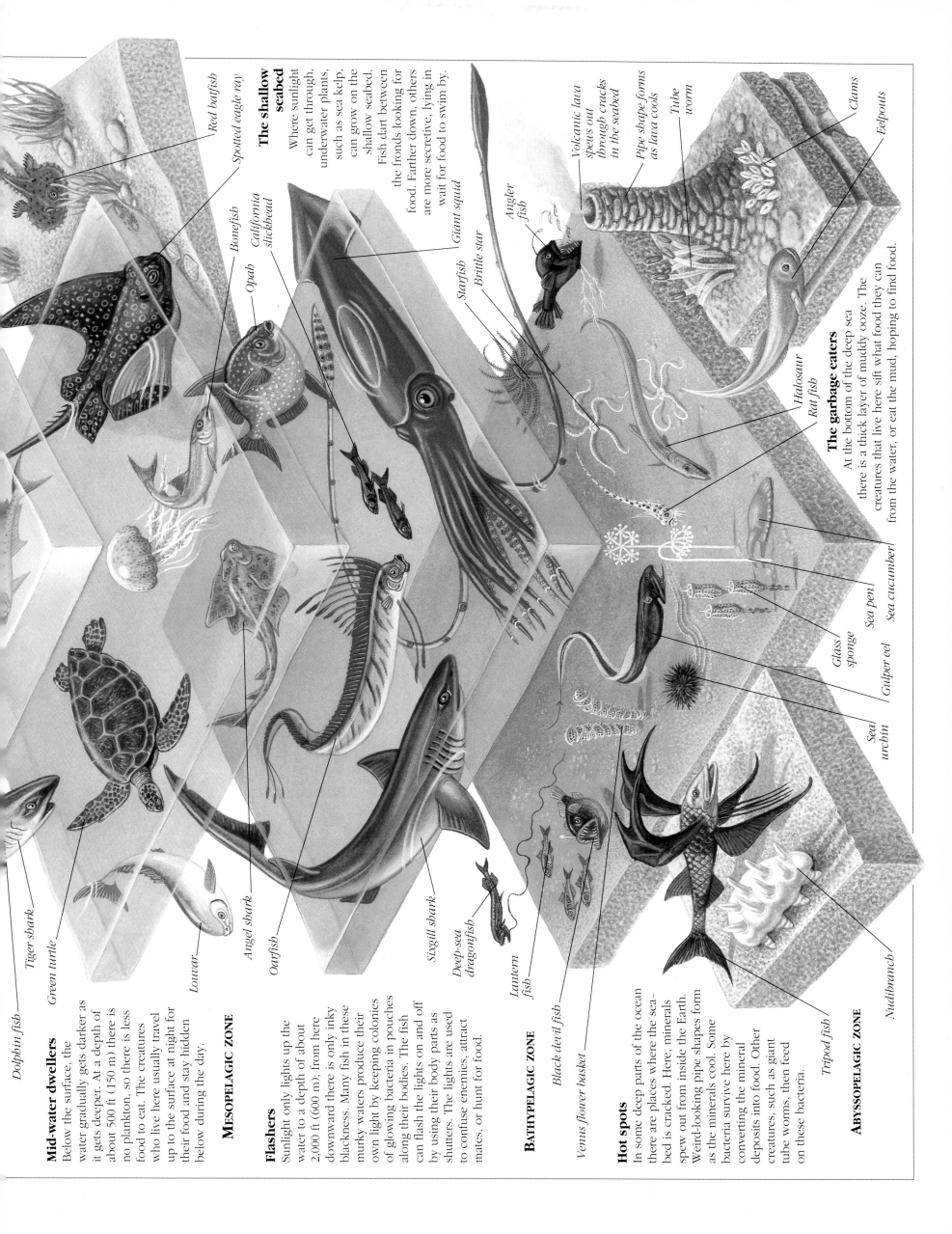

Red batfish

Spotted eagle ray

The shallow seabed

Where sunlight can get through, underwater plants, such as sea kelp, can grow on the shallow seabed. Fish dart between the fronds looking for food. Farther down, others are more secretive, lying in wait for food to swim by.

Bonefish

Opah

California slickhead

Giant squid

Starfish

Brittle star

Angler fish

Volcanic lava spews out through cracks in the seabed

Pipe shape forms as lava cools

Tube worm

Clams

Eelpouts

Halosaur

Rat fish

The garbage eaters

At the bottom of the deep sea there is a thick layer of muddy ooze. The creatures that live here sift what food they can from the water, or eat the mud, hoping to find food.

Sea pen

Sea cucumber

Glass sponge

Gulper eel

Sea urchin

Nudibranch

Tripod fish

Mid-water dwellers

Below the surface, the water gradually gets darker as it gets deeper. At a depth of about 500 ft (150 m) there is no plankton, so there is less food to eat. The creatures who live here usually travel up to the surface at night for their food and stay hidden below during the day.

Dolphin fish

Tiger shark

Green turtle

Louvar

MESOPELAGIC ZONE

Flashers

Sunlight only lights up the water to a depth of about 2,000 ft (600 m); from here downward there is only inky blackness. Many fish in these murky waters produce their own light by keeping colonies of glowing bacteria in pouches along their bodies. The fish can flash the lights on and off by using their body parts as shutters. The lights are used to confuse enemies, attract mates, or hunt for food.

Angel shark

Oarfish

Sixgill shark

Deep-sea dragonfish

Lantern fish

BATHYPELAGIC ZONE

Black devil fish

Venus flower basket

Hot spots

In some deep parts of the ocean there are places where the sea-bed is cracked. Here, minerals spew out from inside the Earth. Weird-looking pipe shapes form as the minerals cool. Some bacteria survive here by converting the mineral deposits into food. Other creatures, such as giant tube worms, then feed on these bacteria.

ABYSSOPELAGIC ZONE

INDEX

ACKNOWLEDGMENTS

Dorling Kindersley would like to thank the following people who helped in the preparation of this book:

Shaila Awan for editorial assistance

Lynn Bresler for the index